Grandma's First Christmas in Heaven!

Written by Judy Billing
Illustrated by Olha Tkachenko

Dedicated to my Karen. Love you forever!

Grandma's First Christmas in Heaven!
Billing, Judy - author, 2022
Illustrations, layout & design by Olha Tkachenko, Little Big Me Publishing, 2022   WWW.LITTLEBIG.ME
ISBN: 978-1-7776036-3-2
All rights © Judy Billing. No part of this publication may be reproduced, stored in retrieval system, or transmitted in any form or by any means: electronic, mechanical, photocopying, recording, or otherwise, without the prior written permission of the author.

Gram was happy in heaven
From the moment she came.
There were no strangers there;
She knew everyone's name.

She ran to see Jesus
When she first came in,
For He was the One
Who had died for her sin.
Such a beautiful moment
As she knelt at His feet
And He lifted her up
In His arms, oh so sweet.

Then she heard a small voice
Say, "Grandma, it's me!"
And her sweet grandson Bobby
Climbed up on her knee.

Oh My! Grandma's heart
Was just bursting with joy!
Lots of smiles, hugs, and kisses
From her sweet little boy!

They went for a walk
And they started to play.
They laughed and they sang.
Such a wonderful day!
There was peace. There was joy.
There was love all around.
No sadness; no tears
In this place would be found.

Then one day Gram noticed
A bit of a change;
More excitement than usual.
How peculiar. How strange.
Grandma took Bobby's hand
And they ran off to see.
What had caused this excitement?
Now what could it be?
There was lots going on.
There was quite a display.
They were all getting ready
To celebrate Christmas Day.

How Grandma loved Christmas!
The best time of year.
People seemed so much happier
Always full of good cheer!

Gram's days were quite busy.
Always so much to do.
There were cookies to bake;
Writing Christmas cards too.

The tree needed trimming
And the wreaths needed hung.
There was door-to-door caroling
With songs to be sung.

A Sunday School pageant
With costumes to sew
And piano recitals
Where Gram loved to go.

But now Gram's in heaven;
Her first Christmas here.
How fun! How exciting!
She grinned ear-to-ear!
This Christmas seemed different;
She knew that it would.
"This is perfect!" thought Grandma.
"This is better than good!"

The angels were joyfully
Preparing the way
For a big celebration
For Jesus' Birthday!

Everyone was rejoicing
More than ever before
For that long-ago birth
Of the One we adore!

All the angels had gathered;
It was really a sight!
Their wings opened wide,
Celebrating this night!
Oh my! Such excitement!
Grandma looked all around.
The night was all filled
With a glorious sound!

The sky was ablaze
With such beautiful hues!
The Archangel appearing
To announce the Big News!
"Our Jesus was born!
His work has been done!
Hallelujah! Praise God
For sending His Son!"

So, stay well my darlings;
I'll always love you.
And never forget
That He loves you all too!

Bake lots of cookies
And have lots of fun,
But always remember
That He is the One…

Who was born Christmas Day
So that we could live here
All together, forever.
You need never fear.
Grandma's happy in heaven;
You'll see her again.
Sending big hugs and kisses!
Merry Christmas! Amen!

CPSIA information can be obtained
at www.ICGtesting.com
Printed in the USA
BVHW021755290422
635753BV00005B/115